LOOK INSIDE

ITALY

Ian James
&
Joy Richardson

Photography by Chris Fairclough

Watts Books

London ● New York ● Sydney

CONTENTS

©1995 Watts Books
96 Leonard Street
London EC2A 4RH

Franklin Watts Australia
14 Mars Road
Lane Cove
NSW 2066

A differentiated text edition of
Inside Italy, first published in 1988.

Design: K & Co

Cover design: Nina Kingsbury

Illustrations: Hayward Art Group

ISBN: 0 7496 1879 5

10 9 8 7 6 5 4 3 2 1

Printed in Belgium

Dewey Decimal Classification:
914.5

A CIP catalogue record for this
book is available from the British
Library.
Additional photographs:
Allsport 19, Zoe Dominic 22(t);
Italian State Tourist Office 5 (t), 21,
22; Mansell Collection 8;
Popperfoto 9;
With thanks to Giorgio Armani 27.

Front cover: James Davis
Travel Photography.

The Land

Italy is a large country in southern Europe.

On the map it looks like a long boot sticking out into the Mediterranean Sea.

The Alps are mountains on the northern border of Italy where it joins the rest of Europe.

Italy also includes two large islands, Sicily and Sardinia.

Below: There are lots of beaches and holiday resorts on Italy's long Mediterranean coastline.

Above: Mount Vesuvius is a famous volcano overlooking the city of Naples.

Left:
The Dolomites are part of the Alps.

Above: There are lakes among the mountains in northern Italy.

There are volcanoes in southern Italy.

Mount Vesuvius erupted in Roman times
and buried the town of Pompeii.
The last time it erupted was fifty years ago.

Southern Italy is dry and hot with mild winters.
The mountainous north has cold winters,
sunny summers and plenty of rain.

The people and their history

Many people have settled in Italy.

The Romans took power around 500 B.C.. They conquered a huge empire and ruled for nearly a thousand years.

They made laws and built cities and roads. There are ruins all over Italy.

Below: The Forum in Rome was the centre of government for the Roman Empire.

After the Romans, Italy was disunited until the 19th century.

City states such as Venice and Florence ruled themselves. They became very wealthy and encouraged great art. Other countries ruled other parts of Italy.

Giuseppe Garibaldi fought hard to unite the country under one king. He helped Victor Emmanuel to become king of Italy in 1861.

Below: Victor Emmanuel (on the white horse) was the first king to rule most of Italy.

8

Above: American troops freed Rome in 1944. Italy then joined the fight against Germany.

Modern Italy has had many changes of government.

The dictator Benito Mussolini ruled Italy from the 1920s. He sided with Hitler in World War II.

In 1948, the Italians voted to become a republic with a president. Italy has lots of political parties. The government keeps changing.

Towns and cities

57 million people live in Italy.

People have moved away from the dry lands of southern Italy into towns and cities.

The northern parts of the country are the most crowded.

The largest cities are Rome, Milan, Naples and Turin.

Below: Many farmers live in villages near their farms.

Left:
The Leaning
Tower of Pisa
attracts many
tourists.

Below: Italian
cities are linked by
high-speed roads.

The old cities are proud of their history.

Naples was once the capital of a large kingdom. Milan and Venice were the capitals of independent city-states.

Venice is a beautiful city. It is built on islands with canals instead of streets. People use boats called gondolas to travel around.

Below: The beautiful city of Venice sits on islands in a lagoon.

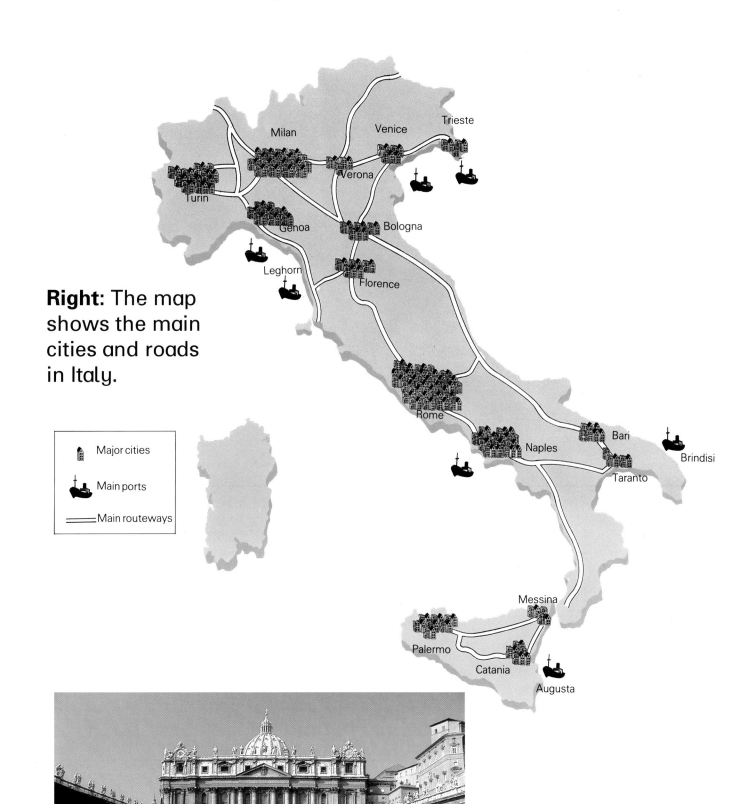

Right: The map shows the main cities and roads in Italy.

Trieste
Venice
Milan
Verona
Turin
Genoa
Bologna
Leghorn
Florence

Major cities
Main ports
Main routeways

Rome
Naples
Bari
Brindisi
Taranto

Messina
Palermo
Catania
Augusta

Left: St Peter's church is in Vatican City in Rome.

13

Rome was once the centre of the Roman Empire.

Now it is the capital city of Italy. It is a busy modern city with many reminders of the past.

Vatican City in Rome is the world's tiniest independent state. It is the headquarters of the Roman Catholic Church. The Pope lives there.

Below: Can you find these places on the plan of Rome?
1 St. Peter's Church
2 Castel Sant' Angelo (a Medieval fortress)
3 Piazza Navona
4 Palazzo Farnese
5 The Pantheon
6 Piazza di Spagna and Spanish Steps
7 Via Vittorio Veneto
8 Ancient Roman ruins
9 The Colosseum

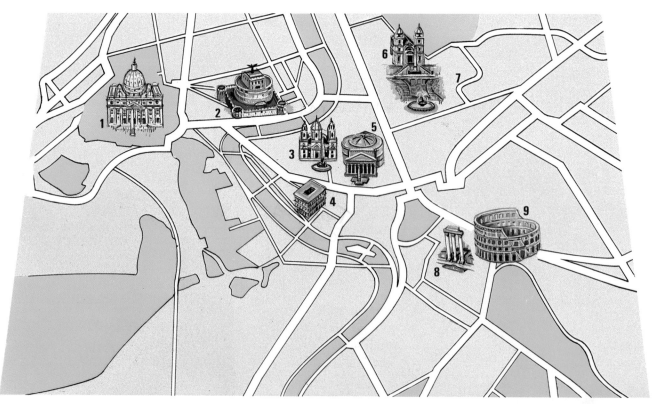

Family life

In the cities, many people live in apartments.

On the edges of cities people live in modern houses with gardens. Most families own a car and a washing machine.

People in the countryside are not so wealthy. There are not so many jobs outside the cities.

Most Italians think family life is very important and keep in close touch with their relatives.

Left: A family outside their apartment block in Turin.

15

Left: Most apartments have balconies where people can dry their washing.

Below: An Italian family in their living room.

Food

Italian pasta is popular worldwide.

Lasagna, macaroni and spaghetti are different types of pasta, all made from flour.

Each part of Italy has its own special dishes. Pizza comes from Naples. Minestrone soup comes from Milan.

Most Italians eat their main meal at lunchtime and have a light dinner in the evening.

Below: Many people buy food in open-air markets or in small shops.

Above: Families get together for meals.

Left:
Meals often start with a dish of mixed pasta.

Sports and pastimes

Italians like watching sport.

Soccer attracts big crowds on Sundays. Many people enjoy fishing, horse-riding, tennis and skiing.

At home, watching television is the most popular pastime.

Some people take foreign holidays. Others like to stay at home or go to the seaside in Italy.

Below: Lots of people support Italy's top soccer teams.

Left: People from all over the world enjoy holidays in Italy's ski resorts.

Below: On Sundays people like to stroll in the parks.

The arts

Many famous artists were Italian.

In the period called the Renaissance, artists such as Leonardo da Vinci and Michelangelo created magnificent works of art.

Italy is known as the home of opera. Famous operas by Verdi and Puccini are played around the world. Many great singers are from Italy.

Below: The magnificent palaces, churches and museums in Florence house great art treasures from the past.

Above: A grand scene from an opera by Verdi being performed in Italy.

Left: Michelangelo painted the ceiling of the Sistine Chapel in the Vatican.

Farming

Italy grows a lot of food.

The richest soil is in the north. The crops grown there include wheat, maize and rice.

Cattle and sheep provide meat and milk. Trees produce almonds, oranges, lemons and olives. Italy supplies many other countries with olives and olive oil.

Grapes are grown all over Italy. The country makes a fifth of the world's wine.

Below: Groves of olive trees in central Italy.

Above: A farmer at work in the fertile Po valley in northern Italy. You can see grape vines in the background.

Left: Italy grows a huge variety of fruits and vegetables. They are sold at home or exported.

Industry

The big industrial cities are in central and northern Italy.

Italy has little fuel of its own so it has to buy oil, gas and coal from abroad. It uses water power to make a quarter of its electricity.

Some minerals come from Italian mines but most are imported.

Italy makes lots of cars. The huge Fiat car company also owns Alfa Romeo and Ferrari.

Below: Fast Italian sports cars are admired all over the world.

Look at the map
to see what is
produced
where in Italy.

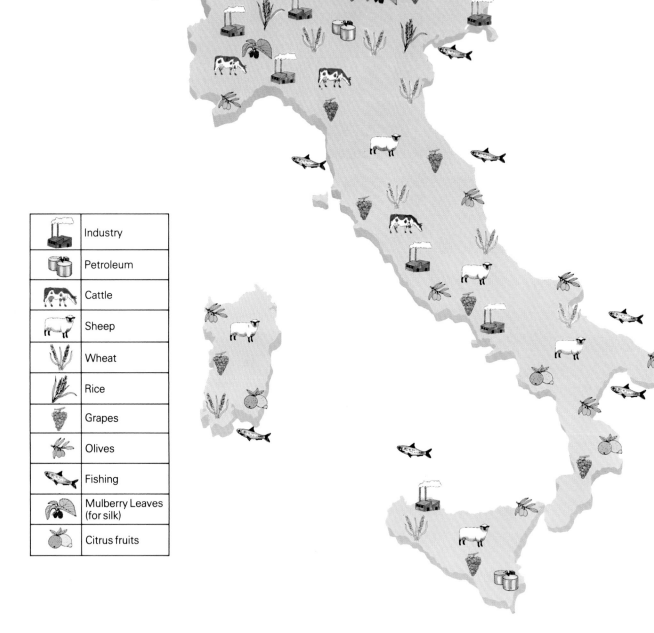

	Industry
	Petroleum
	Cattle
	Sheep
	Wheat
	Rice
	Grapes
	Olives
	Fishing
	Mulberry Leaves (for silk)
	Citrus fruits

Florence, Milan and Rome are major cities in the clothing industry.

Italian clothes are sold all over the world. They are known for their elegant looks and good quality.

Italian leather is used to make shoes and handbags, and wool is used for elegant knitwear and smart suits.

Left: Giorgio Armani is famous for the high quality, beautiful clothes he designs.

Looking to the future

Italy has been growing richer.

Italy used to be quite a poor country, troubled by terrorism and political changes.

In the last twenty years, industry has grown and tourism has increased.

Now Italy is one of the richest countries in the European Union.

Below: Children at school in Turin have a bright future.

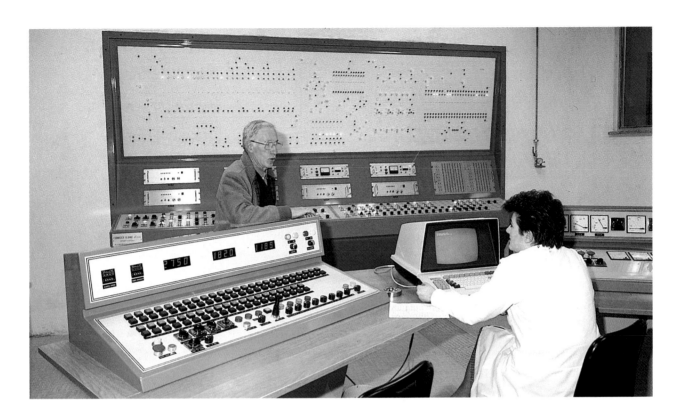

Above: Italy has many high-technology industries.

Italy is working to solve its problems.

Southern parts of the country which have little industry are still poor. Growing industry is polluting the cities.

Italy is developing new technology. It is looking to the future.

Facts about Italy

Area:
301,225 sq km
(116,304 sq miles)

Population:
57,235,000 (1993
est)

Capital:
Rome

Largest cities:
Rome (population
2,791,000)
Milan (1,432,000)
Naples (1,206,000)
Turin (992,000)
Palmero (734,000)
Genoa (701,000)

Official language:
Italian

Religion:
Christianity

Main exports:
Textiles,
chemicals,
footwear, iron and
steel, machinery,
vehicles

Unit of currency:
Lira

Italy compared with other countries

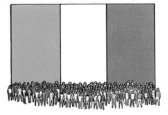
Italy 190 per sq. km

Britain 238 per sq. km

USA 27 per sq. km.

Australia 2 per sq. km.

Above: How many people?
Italy is heavily populated
compared with some other
countries.

Below: How large? Italy has
a small land area compared
with some countries.

USA

Australia

Italy   **UK**

Below: Italian money and stamps.

Index